Dr Elise,
Thank you so much for
your support and for being
such a blessing to so many?
God is using you for his plan.

Stay inspiring!

Mel

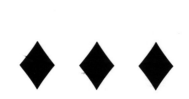

Reflections of Life

A Collection of Poetry, Prose and Images

POWERED
PUBLISHING

Reflections of Life, A Collection of Poetry, Prose and Images

Copyright © 2018 by Mel Brown McGinnis

ISBN: 978-0-692-14532-6

Published by
Mpowered Sports and Entertainment, LLC
dba MPowered Publishing
P.O. Box 183841
Arlington, Texas 76096

Printed in the United States of America

Except as otherwise noted, all text, poems, images and photos featured in *Reflections of Life* are the original work of Mel Brown McGinnis.

Cover Illustrations: Mel Brown McGinnis

Cover Design: Ginaona Habeebulaah

Back Cover Photographer: Sandra Hill

Dedication

To my husband, you are the blessing from God that allows me to walk in my truth. Thank you for supporting my dreams and encouraging me to dance!

To my family and friends, thank you for always supporting me, believing in me, and encouraging me to live my purpose as God intended.

To my mother, my grandmothers, my aunts, my sisters, and my sorority sisters, thank you for always pouring into me. You are the reason I am. I will always pay it forward so that those that come after me have the opportunity to shine bright like diamonds!

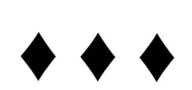

Acknowledgments

I am first a child of God, and every fiber of my being believes that I can do all things through Christ who strengthens me.

I am so humbled and grateful that God has given me the ability to write verse, but more importantly he has given me the courage to tell this part of my story. I believe this work has come to fruition because it was a part of God's plan so as a child of God, I proceed accordingly.

I acknowledge the journey that I have traveled to get to this point. It has required me to stretch my mind and think outside of what I have always known in order to survive.

Thank you to my first line of defense, Ieisha, Michelle, Leann, Melinda, Jennifer, Angie, Alicia, and Dr. Samone. Your support and insight are invaluable. I can't express my gratitude enough. I appreciate each of you more than you know.

I pray this collection will help others to see that no matter how hard life gets, and no matter the challenges you face, there is light at the end of the tunnel. If you trust in God's plan for your life, you will come out on the other side of the journey... refreshed, renewed, and ready to take your place in the world!

Inside The Pages

Table of Contents

INTRODUCTION   **1**

CHAPTER 1: HER DIAMONDS   **3**

    #AndGodCreatedWoman   5
    #diamondgirl   9
    Into The Light   11

CHAPTER 2: BROKEN   **15**

    Shattered Glass   17
    Seasons   21
    Addiction 25
    Breathe 29

CHAPTER 3: RELATIONSHIP R&R   **33**

    Relationship R&R   35
    The Room   41

CHAPTER 4: PRINCE OF HEARTS   **45**

    Rendition   47
    Rendition Complete   49
    My Purple Heart   57

CHAPTER 5: THIS AMERICA   63

Providence   65
Of Kings and Presidents   75

CHAPTER 6: MY BROTHER, MY SISTER,   81
MY KEEPER

To Heaven's Angel   83
CRAZY.has.a.name   87

CHAPTER 7: THE GAME   93

FANatic   95
To the Athlete in the Zone   97

CHAPTER 8: FAMILY TIES   103

Faces of Life   105

CHAPTER 9: YOUR REFLECTIONS   109

Foreword

When we first met, almost 20 years ago now, Mel and I were twenty-somethings navigating the corridors of law school. As we tend to be early in life, we were stubborn, young, ready to take on the world and secure, maybe too secure, in the knowledge that we knew exactly what we wanted.

We became fast friends partly because we quickly discovered that, not only did we have similar interests, but we had similar paths. We were inspired by the law, lovers of the written word, and seekers of the evidence of the beauty in this world. As we continued to be friends over the years, we watched those commonalities intersect and culminate in the most remarkable ways.

During law school, we strived to create the same life that most people, in the beginning, attempted to create. We wanted a life filled with love, happiness, family and intellectually challenging careers. Though we knew we had a lot to look forward to, we still managed to think that we had been through it all.

But, of course, we were wrong. We had not really been through anything.

We had not experienced heartbreak so deep that recovering meant not only protecting our severely damaged hearts, but also preventing it from irreparably damaging our souls. We had not yet experienced the shock of learning that a passionate, all-encompassing, would-do-anything-for-you type of love could, either literally or figuratively, force you into making the most heartbreaking of decisions... "my life or yours." We were astute enough to know where we came from, but too naive to give the proper reverence and respect to that place, that time and those ancestors. And, we could not even contemplate the anguish associated with loss of the person, a stranger, that provided the soundtrack to the most instrumental moments of our lives.

Reflections is, quite simply, a glimpse into the life of Mel Brown McGinnis. It is about the above-mentioned experiences and the lens through which she sees the world as a result of them. At times, it is about getting on the other side of turbulent emotions and putting them in their proper place. At other times, it's about working hard to allow herself to feel emotions that should stay right there in that place. In pictures and in beautiful prose, she opens her heart and gently guides us through her story. The pictures are varied and splendid. Some showcase nature in unique and innumerable forms. Others are paintings created by the author herself. And, still others are pictures taken with, taken of or taken by the author in the midst of significant moments in her life. Each poem allows the reader to walk with her through growth, transition, perceived failure, loneliness, nostalgia, acceptance and love.

The goal of *Reflections* is not to be preachy. It is to share her experiences in a way that stimulates the reader into feeling entertained in one moment and analytical during the next, comforted during one moment and enraged in yet another.

Reflections is a testament to our strength as human beings and an ode to our capacity to rise, self-reflect, and love again. At times, it is also an indictment of our capacity to hate.

Aptly entitled *Reflections*, it offers the reader and the author the peace and understanding that often comes from a backwards glance at life. It offers hope to the reader who would ask: "why me?" and optimism to the reader who may be asking "why not me yet?"

It's been said that we live life looking forward, but we understand it looking backwards. What *Reflections* provides to the reader is a reminder that the journey may, in fact, be worth it, that this world is beautiful and that love, in whatever form, exists if you want it.

Several of the pictures and poems spoke to my soul in ways that only great artistry can do. They left me with a feeling that maybe, just maybe things – the good, the bad and the ugly- work out exactly as they are meant to.

I think that one of those poems, if not all of them, will do the same for you.

Michelle D. Craig, J.D., BCL
Owner/Founder of Transcendent Law Group and Prosquire
Managing Law Firm Partner, Writer and lover of words
New Orleans, LA.

To The Reader

Thank you for deciding to take this journey with me!

This collection of poetry, prose, and images is just that...a collection. It is intended to provide different perspectives on many different topics, but at the same time provide a cohesive experience for the reader. Over the last 10 years, I have made a 360 turnaround from just being alive, to living!

This collection represents many experiences that I've had in my life, but it also represents the experiences of others as I attempt to provide a path to acceptance of the past, transition to the present, and starting anew for a bright future. It is my hope that you will be able to relate to the poetry, prose and images in some way. Even though a certain poem or work of prose may not be your story, it may be your mother's story, or your sister's story, or your brother's story, or even your child or best friend's story.

Each chapter is composed to encourage reflection on a different topic and how it relates to your life or simply to the world today. Since I could never fit my works into a nice little "genre" box, each chapter also contains a photograph that tells a part of the story, many of which are from my *Natural Elements* photo collection as I fancy myself an amateur photographer. As I tell each story through poetry, the goal is to provide insight on how the photo relates to the poem and why I chose each photo for that particular chapter.

This work intentionally explores a variety of topics to stimulate your mind and your heart. Writing is the spice of life and this collection has something to which everyone can relate. Whether the topic is empowering women, finding that forever love after a failed relationship, looking through the lens of violence, paying tribute to the life of a musical legend, succeeding in life despite humble beginnings, or commentary on the political landscape of our country, my hope is that as the reader, you gain a different perspective on how poetry, prose and images can work together to tell a story.

I credit my friend and sorority sister, the amazing, awesomely talented, best-selling author, Angie Ransome Jones, for giving me the idea of combining my expressions of love into a single work! This collection is my truth. I encourage you to read it individually, or as a group and reflect on how you can use my experiences to help you in your life or maybe to help someone else.

When I was in that dark place trying to find my way out, my sister from another mother encouraged me to seek professional help because honestly I couldn't see my way through it on my own. So twice a month for twelve months, I had *"conversations from the white sofa,"* with my therapist. My therapist helped me through those dark months, and she also helped me to develop tools that I could use going forward so that I would not fall back into those habits that led me to the dark place.

The end of each chapter contains questions that are designed to "start the conversation" in hopes that thinking things through critically and talking about difficult issues will help someone else the way it helped me. It is an incredible joy to be a blessing to others. I pray that you are blessed by my story.

So let's talk!

In the Beginning ...

The Poetry...

The Prose...

The Images...

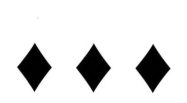

Introduction

I fell in love with poetry in Ms. Tucker's 9th grade English class. As I recited one of my favorite poems, *Birches*, by Robert Frost, I could hear Ms. Tucker's voice in my head saying "pronounciate, enunciate, and make me feel what you're reading!" Ms. Tucker is not a teacher that you EVER forget! Famous amongst her students for her unique delivery of literary devices such as onomatopoeia and alliteration, her approach was admirable because keeping 14 year olds engaged in English literature was no small feat. But she held my attention all year long...and so did poetry.

My love for writing was solidified when I was 15, and I wrote two poems that were published in my 10th grade Honors English literary magazine. One was about love, the other, rather tellingly, was titled "America." Both juvenile in the maturity of the writing, but meaningful and relevant for the time...and yet still relevant today. I've been writing most of the days of my life in some form since that time.

I have always wanted to publish a full-length literary work, but I always thought my maiden offering would be in the form of a novel with fictional characters who lived in a fictional place somewhere in a small town in Mississippi.

Because of the personal nature of poetry, I never imagined that my debut literary work would be my very own collection of poetry and prose that is so close to my heart I can feel it beating. But that is what God put on my heart to bring you...

So here it is, in its rarest, purest, most authentic form...to tell my story. So prepare to take this journey with me...and be prepared to dance!

"Walk in Your Purpose,
Live in
Your Truth."

Chapter 1 ... Her Diamonds

Empowering women to shine bright like diamonds!
Find that thing in life that moves you ...
and then dance for it!

#thefutureisfemale

"Glacier Falls"
Photo: Anchorage, Alaska

"Glacier Falls" is a photo of a waterfall in Alaska that was so beautiful I almost couldn't believe my eyes. I chose to include it in this collection because it reminds me of all the things a woman has to be … she has to be soft and nurturing like the water but at the same time she has to be hardened like the rock to withstand many of the challenges in life… and she has to shine like a diamond, in living up to society's jaded view of beauty. But the true spirit of a woman is personified in the phrase when you find that thing in life that excites you and that you're passionate about, go after it 110% with all your heart…and then dance for it…shine bright like a diamond…that is the true beauty of a woman.

#AndGodCreatedWoman

she is woman...hear her R.O.A.R.
to the highest heights
just watch her soar

she honors her roots
but embraces her wings
she equally balances life's big moments
with the little things

she's created by God
so dismissing her contributions
would be tragic
she exudes #girlpower she #slays
for all the world to see her #diamondgirlmagic ...

she is woman...hear her R.O.A.R.
she has taken her seat at the table
no longer will she accept closed doors

she believes in she.and.us.and.we
by her very existence God said
the world is better with diversity

she is fierce, she is loyal, she is undoubtedly free

open your eyes she is woman
and God created her for thee

she shines brightly
like clear diamonds indeed
to be in her presence
is to experience the rarified air she breathes

the world requires her greatness
and tenderness yet the same

she's a princess cut diamond
woman is her God-given name

she conceals her tears
she faces the years
with knowledge that she has to be better than him

boldness is her nature
you can never steal her 4 carat shine
she's created by God
and now is her time

you will certainly be in awe
of the stories she will inspire others to tell
she's created by God
the future is female

when life breaks her down
she rebuilds and comes back for more
she's the color of diamond
she is woman… HEAR HER R.O.A.R!

"Yellow Rose of Truth"
Photo: Long Beach, California

I took this photo in Long Beach, California. A yellow rose symbolizes happiness, friendship, joy and truth. I don't have a daughter, but if I did, I would want her to know that it's ok to live in her truth. So many of our young ladies today have issues with self-esteem because of the unrealistic societal view of "pretty" that we have created. I want all young ladies to know that they are "diamondgirls" and they are strong and beautiful, and it's enough to just be who you are…you are enough.

#diamondgirl

To "Be" a #diamondgirl is to…
Be adventurous
Be assertive
Be beautiful
Be bold
Be brave
Be bright
Be clever
Be faithful
Be fearless
Be flexible
Be grateful
Be independent
Be joyful
Be kind
Be knowledgeable
Be loving
Be loyal
Be respectful
Be shiny
Be strong
Be truthful
Be wise
…but mostly just.Be.YOU…
You are enough.

"Desert Beauty"
Photo: Desert, Dubai UAE

I am a proud member of Alpha Kappa Alpha Sorority, Inc. Membership in this illustrious organization is an honor and a privilege. To be a woman of Alpha Kappa Alpha is simply to love her. I chose "Desert Beauty" because of the amazing sunlight that covers the gorgeous desert in Dubai/ UAE. I took this photo on a desert safari in Dubai. This picture doesn't do justice to the beauty of this part of the world, but this desert reminds me of the make-up of an Alpha Kappa Alpha woman...she lights the sky with her classic, layered, cultured beauty, inside and out.

Into The Light

...for my sisters of Alpha Kappa Alpha Sorority, Inc.

Out of the darkness
Into the light
Comes Alpha Kappa Alpha
When she steps into the place
You are clearly in the presence of
Royalty, style and grace
Her smile lights up the night
Her fierceness sets the world on fire

Out of the darkness
Into the light
She *breathes* Alpha Kappa Alpha
She exudes sisterliness, courage, and strength of will
Her sacrifice ... magnificent
In her moment time stands still

She is a woman of faith
Her vision ... profound
Her heart is made of pearls
It loves without bounds

Out of the darkness
Into the light
She *bleeds* Alpha Kappa Alpha
She was born to make others great
Service, scholarship and excellence are in her DNA

She gives freely of her time and skills
Her convictions ... admirable
Her commitment ... never ends

Out of the darkness
Into the light

She *lives* Alpha Kappa Alpha

Her love … she gives
Her heart … she gives
Her time … she gives
Her all … she gives

For *her* Alpha Kappa Alpha still

The many hours
You may never know
She never complains
Does it all with a sisterly flow

Out of the darkness
Into the light
She *works* for Alpha Kappa Alpha

No matter when you said her vows
3 weeks, 3 years, 3 decades ago
She grabs you by your soul
She never lets go

Forever Alpha Kappa Alpha

Her beauty … timeless
Her spirit … timeless
Her pretty girl … timeless
Her 20 pearls … timeless
Her ivy stance … timeless
Her flawlessness … timeless
Her pinky to the sky … timeless
Her skee-wee … like mine … timeless

Out of the darkness
Into the AKAlight
Her infectious smile lights the night
To her heart's pink and green delight
She *is* Alpha Kappa Alpha…
Recognize.

Reflections

Conversations from the White Sofa...

1. What are your thoughts on the modern women's movement and how are the roles of women in leadership positions different in today's society?

2. What can you do to support and empower women to reach leadership positions?

3. What values do you think are important to instill in young girls to encourage them to be the future leaders of tomorrow?

_____

_____

_____

_____

_____

_____

_____

_____

_____

_____

_____

_____

_____

_____

_____

_____

_____

_____

_____

_____

*"Pay Attention to the Message,
Not the Messenger."*

Chapter 2 ... Broken

*The moments that shatter you are a part of
your life's story...they are not to be erased...they are
moments from which you learn...and move on.*

*Heartache has the ability to suffocate your spirit.
Find your peace in God's creations and
He will allow you to breathe.*

*This chapter is about being broken and trusting in God to
provide that solace and allow you to rebuild and put the
pieces back together.*

"Shattered Glass"
Photo: A Sad Night in Texas

This picture is from a time in my life where I was working through the after effects of a failed marriage. This shattered glass is what remained on the day it all came crashing down. I am including this here because this moment began a series of events that truly shaped who I am today. Finding inner strength to continue after you've been broken is a blessing from God. This photo no longer moves me…but it is a part of my story… not to be erased…but a moment from which to learn.

Shattered Glass

A million pieces lay on the floor for a week
The fractured reflection stares back at me
The sadness consumes me
The image of unbreakable love
Weakened by life and other things we will never know of…

I can no longer endure the pain
The lessons of betrayal from the past
My eyes blood red from tears
My heart…shattered…like glass…

My spirit deathly broken
Partially, at my own hand
The love we once shared for an eternity
Sinking deathly like quick sand…

I can no longer endure the pain
The lessons of betrayal from the past
My eyes glisten wet from tears
My heart…shattered…like glass…

I want…to want to love you again
But my heart sees it differently
That once sacred time has passed us by
Now you must let me be free…

I can no longer endure the pain
The lessons of betrayal from the past
My eyes swollen from tears
My heart…shattered…like glass…

You deserve a love to fill your heart
To provide the laughter of children that you need…

I thought our love would be a novel
I now know it was only a short story.

God, please help me stop the pain
Please forgive us for our betrayals of the past
No more tears, no more fears…

Only shattered glass.

"Blades of Grass"
Photo: Long Beach, California

When you're in a dark place and you don't understand how to escape the sadness, have faith that God will send an angel to tell you what he needs you to hear. It may be in the simplest form, like "Blades of Grass," a natural element in which you might never expect to find beauty. You may not even recognize it until the seasons change, and the brown grass turns green. But pay attention to God's message, not the messenger. I was in a dark place for years, but had to learn that all of God's creations are beautiful and deserving of life…including me.

Seasons

There was a time when I could not see beyond the grief
The sadness and fear and despair ran forever deep
I often wondered if I could make my world better
By writing those whom I loved a letter
And letting life move along without me
If that was the only way my soul would truly be free...

Free from the darkness, chaos, and disappointment
And not living up to expectations that I had placed upon me
Expectations are heavy if you live at my level
And that day I failed to cope
With this journey greatly unsettled.

So as I had done so many times night after night
I once again asked God to show me the light
That was the only thing left for me to do
If I was to survive *that* night and make it through
And by His grace the sun shone through to light the way
And I smiled because I know God sent me an angel that day.

I could breathe again and was no longer afraid to see
What God had in store for me and what could truly be
He knew there was only a certain love I would receive
So He sent me the one angel that could make me believe
That my life was worth living
Tears of sadness could be joy
And wipe away the coldness that filled me with sorrow...

I could hear the laughter, the love and peace within
And unbeknownst to you, I placed my heart in your hands
Your love was like a volcano
That erupted and rushed all over me

And I knew that it was because of you
That I would finally be free

Free to live my life and be who God intended
So that I would understand my plans had to be His plans
Until the day it ended...

Today there are tears, but for a different reason
Because I know God allowed me
To borrow you only for a season
I admire you being who you promised to be
As I will forever be grateful to you for loving me.

I now know that God's love is forever true
And He sent His blessings to me through you
God sent me an angel today
To laugh, to love, to smile to pray
So I thank Him for allowing me to live life
And reap blessings from above
You will forever be my angel equal in passion and in love.

"Shells on Blackbeard"
Photo: Blackbeard Island, Caribbean

Addiction comes in all forms, and can be a detriment and a blessing at the same time...addiction can be satisfying and overwhelming, sinful and all forgiving, and can bring you peace and chaos in the same space of 60 seconds, which is what this photo represents to me...the peace and tranquility of seashells on the beach, but also the sharp edges of the shells that will cut you if you're not in control...control your addictions...or they will control you...

Addiction

One o'clock, one twenty two, one thirty seven, one fifty eight...am

Two eleven, two thirty three, two forty, two fifty five...am
I stare at the clock with red numbers beside my bed
As I watch each minute tick away...I can't sleep
This is the random, yet constant, hourly cycle
Where you are the star of the show
The thought of you plays over and over and over in my mind
The rush, the fire, the intensity takes over...I am addicted.

Driving in my car, I think of you
Walking up the stairs, I think of you
You are my very first thought as I wake
I feel the intensity of you in my dreams
The thought of you plays over and over and over in my mind
The rush, the fire, the intensity takes over...I am addicted.

You are the one in my dreams
Yet so far away from possible
God must be playing a cruel joke on me
To put you in front of me as the answer
Yet when I reach out to touch you, you're not there.

But tonight, I see you, I touch you, I feel you
The intensity of you is overwhelming

The truth of you plays over and over and over on my skin
The rush, the fire, the intensity has taken over...
I am addicted.

You are everywhere, you feel up the room,
You fill up my mind
My body dripping wet from the inferno that is you

I now realize you *are* the rush, you *are* the fire,
You *are* the intensity…I am addicted…to you.

For hours, I touch you, I feel you,
The depth of you reaches inside
The power, the force, the desire, the intensity
That is you fills me
I can't control it, the room is spinning, the earth is shaking…inhale…
exhale…satisfaction.

Three o'clock, three twenty two, three thirty seven,
Three fifty eight…am

Four eleven, four thirty three, four forty, four fifty five…am
The thought of you plays over and over and over in my mind
The rush, the fire, the intensity takes over
I need you again…

I am addicted.

"Flight of the Pacific"
Photo: Pacific Coast Highway, California

I climbed up on a rock on the banks of the Pacific Ocean during a tour down the PCH to get this photo. I caught the bird freely flying across the ocean in my shot and it instantly brought me peace. I was dealing with the pain of divorce and this was one of those photos that I always looked back on to bring me peace. I see God's house of love as nature and the beauty of God's natural elements forever amazes me. I see this and know that in spite of the heartache, God will surround you with his love, and at the end of the day, you will be able to breathe.

Breathe

Sadness still consumes me
Loneliness is my only companion
Restless is my true friend
Because love no longer lives here.

My tears keep me company
Pain is the voice in my head
Coping has eluded me
Still love no longer lives here.

Anxiety screams through my skin
The silent cries are deafening
The labored breathing steals my peace
And love no longer lives here.

But God's gift of nature comforts me
For a moment I can breathe
Smiling through the heartache
God's house of love has found me.

For a moment, I can breathe…
In this moment, I am breathing…
I breathe…and breath again.

I am FREE…

Reflections

Conversations from the White Sofa...

1. What do you think you deserve in life?

2. Establish between 5-10 goals for yourself this year and share with the group (or a friend who will hold you accountable).

3. What have you done for yourself today in order to be inspired or to achieve a goal you may have set?

_____

_____

_____

_____

_____

_____

_____

_____

_____

_____

_____

_____

_____

_____

_____

_____

_____

_____

_____

_____

_____

_____

"My Heart Loves Without Bounds. My Soul is at Peace."

Chapter 3 ...
Relationship R & R

After a divorce or a failed relationship, it's hard to find that thing inside you that allows you to trust someone else with your heart. But most people desire meaningful companionship and don't want to spend their lives alone. The key to R&R is to accept the past and move on from it ("recover"), and do your best to understand who you are and what you truly want out of life ("re-learn").

Mastering the often impossible task of truly knowing yourself cuts out a lot of the unnecessary shenanigans in the R&R process so that if you have a choice between some other person and the hubby or wife to-be, you will be prepared to tell the difference.

"Keys to My Soul"
Photo: My Typewriter

After divorce, one of the greatest gifts from God came in the form of my forever love. I had never really known true love until God blessed me with him. The next pieces are inspired by my love for my husband and understanding what it means to be prepared for the blessing of love when God presents it to you. This is a picture of my typewriter that my husband gifted me for Christmas. I call it the "BEST.GIFT.EVER..." and #20 on #thelist tells you why.

Relationship R & R

In my attempts to recover from a failed marriage, I wasn't sure if I ever wanted to be married again, but I was 100% sure I wanted no parts of being alone for the rest of my life either. So I had to "recover" from the relationship blues and "re-learn" healthy relationship behaviors (my version of grown folks "R&R"). Understanding that I had to accept responsibility for the part I played in my previous marriage failing, I knew I had to learn how to actually just be ok with being me before I could even think about a new relationship.

Not that I was eager to jump into another relationship, but as a part of discovering myself, I knew I needed a plan for my life after getting on the other side of divorce. And that plan included how to turn "me" into "we!" Just sitting around hoping it would all work out one day is not really in my nature. It was important to me that I did everything possible not to let mistakes that I made from the past be visited on the present or the future.

I'm not ashamed to admit that a part of my recovery from the relationship blues included a full year of counseling (which I always thought was only for weak individuals…I was wrong). Counseling really helped me to understand myself, but also gain a true understanding of what really matters in a relationship.

What follows are my "20 keys to Recovering and Re-learning healthy relationship behaviors for turning me into we!" These tips have helped me maintain an immensely successful relationship with the man who is now my husband, but more importantly allowed me to be mentally, physically, emotionally and financially prepared to receive the blessing of him…which is what really counts…because opportunity means nothing if you're not ready for it!

Note: this list assumes things such as love, being faithful, loyalty, etc are present and don't need to be said … . ☺

1. **#makeyourlist**—Be honest with yourself and write down those things that you truly, truly want in a relationship, but don't be so inflexible that you miss the forest for the trees … write down the must haves, the things you're flexible on,

and the deal breakers…but remember no one is perfect…not even you (I was blessed to get 39 out of the 40 things on my list…and no I won't tell you what #40 is lol!)

2. **Be open to receive the blessing**—Don't be so angry or bitter that you miss the blessing right in front of you. No one wants to hear every other word about how horrible all men or all women are…bitterness is not attractive.

3. **Your Significant Other (S/O) is not a mind reader**—Don't expect him or her to be. Don't just assume that your S/O knows how you feel about something if you haven't discussed it previously.

4. **You can't be a 4 and want your S/O to be a 10**— A little self-reflection and understanding of your level of physical, mental, emotional and financial well-being is critical. You attract what you are.

5. **Don't make your relationship a cling fest or a control fest!**—It simply doesn't work for men or women.

6. **Be his or her safest place**—Your S/O should be comfortable enough to talk to you about anything without criticism, ridicule or fear of rejection. Never make your S/O feel inferior. Just as important, don't share information with your family or friends about your intimate life with your S/O…that includes financial intimacy. Your business with your S/O is just that…your business.

7. **Be financially intimate**—Financial issues are the leading cause of divorce in America. First, make sure your financial house is in order before you even think about combining with someone else. If you can't take care of you and yours, don't expect someone else to. When you find that person you want to be in a true relationship with, you absolutely MUST be on the same page with your S/O in terms of how you approach finances. Find what works for you both and stick to that. Be financially responsible to each other. Try the 4 accounts approach: one account for the household, one account for him, one account for her, and a joint savings account.

8. **Don't visit your past on your present**—The person you are in a relationship with now is not the person you used to be in a relationship with ... don't treat them like they are. Give them the respect of allowing your current relationship to stand on its own.

9. **Stop looking for the perfect package**—If you can't get past the wrapping you will never get to the gift! Reprogram your mind and remove the words "my type" from your vocabulary. Your future might not be wrapped up in "this height, that weight, this eye color, that hair color, has this job, drives that car, lives in this neighborhood" little box you've always thought he or she might be wrapped in... so be open to someone different or something new ☺

10. **Learn to compromise**—You can't always have everything your way. It's ok to disagree, but you have to guard against silly things becoming arguments. Ask yourself "will this matter 30 days from now?" If not, it's not worth arguing about. Learn to meet each other in the middle on differences.

11. **Be present in your relationship**—Put down the cell phone, turn off the tv, put down the laptop, and be present with your S/O. Pick a time or activity that you will always do together each day and do that.

12. **Put in the time**—It's just that simple. You can't give the best of yourself to everyone and everything else and then leave the "tired worn out you" for your S/O.

13. **Make your relationship a priority**—Others can wait!

14. **Don't be afraid to be his or her fantasy**— if you won't, someone else will.

15. **Don't be jealous of the relationships** they have with their family, the boys or the girls, or the "girl" friends or the "boy" friends.

16. **Don't breach your contract**—A relationship is a contract. If you say you're going to do something, then do that and hold up your end of the deal.

17. **Don't make your relationship about material things**— Your S/O shouldn't be made to feel that he or she has to buy your affection—it won't last.

18. **Find common ground and set joint goals for your relationship**—Highlight those things in your relationship that you both enjoy and look for opportunities to share those things consistently. Set joint goals for your life together and for your relationship, and then work together to achieve those goals.

19. **Be his wife not his mother ... or her husband not her father** ... They both come equipped with one of these.

20. **Be your S/O's biggest fan!** Always support their dreams and let them support yours. This sounds like a simple tip, but besides finances, this is one of the biggest mistakes made in relationships... trying to change someone. Dreams sustain who we are at the heart of things. If you're living a life where your S/O is always attempting to suppress your dreams and wanting you to be someone you're not, that is called settling... and it will never work. If your S/O wants to do something, as long as it's legal, moral and ethical and won't be a detriment to your household, be supportive. It will matter in the end.

These tips helped me to just be a better person. If I had never met my husband, I would have been good. There is absolutely nothing wrong with being single. But I'm so glad that I did meet him and that I was ready for him when he came along. I had a plan to make sure I was worthy of a man like him and that I was also able to recognize if he was deserving of me.

I took the journey for what it really was, and that was helping me to understand who I really am and what I wanted out of my life ... so that if I had a choice between some other guy and hubby-to-be, I could tell the difference. One last thing. One of the most important things on my list was that I wanted a partner who would let me be me and I found that in *him*...

"Reflection"
Photo: Wedding Day, Paris France

This picture says a thousand words. We had many gorgeous photos from our wedding in Paris, France, and our wedding reception, but I chose this photo because as I was standing in front of the mirror, I had an amazing moment of reflection and everything came full circle...I finally liked the person in the mirror staring back at me. "She's me, and she's happy, and I planned for her, and I worked for her, and she's about to marry the love of our life!" This photo captures the essence of what this poem was meant to convey...I love my husband...our love is true, and pure, and I still get butterflies when he walks in the room...

The Room

The flickering candles light the clear night sky
As I sit and talk to God, I ask him "who is this guy?"
Did you really send me someone so perfect for me?
Of course I will obey but my suspicious heart proceeds with caution
you see.

He's tall, he's handsome
Girl he's a Kappa man
Surely he cannot be this perfect
But he checks 39 of my 40 boxes
You understand?

This new love excites me
My heart flutters as the butterflies in my stomach
Dance to our tune
He walks in, he moves close to me
Be still…be still…he's in the room.

It's been six months now,
I blink and a year has passed
I suppress that nervous energy
Because I don't want to move too fast.

In silence I dream of the possibility
Of a lifetime with this man

It's been two years now
But he'll ask me if he wants my hand.

He continues to woo me
Not with gifts or bling or things of that kind
You see I'm a different kind of chic
So I'm turned on by his actions and his mind

Ooooh his intelligence excites me
Because he has to be on my level
I need a man who can talk to me about politics, the Cowboys my 401K
and the Young and the Restless.

We go along with each other's flow
We've settled in nicely, everything is easy
Oh sure there are times when we disagree
But arguments are never needed.

Our foundation is solid, we are lock step and in tune
Every time he walks in, he moves close to me
My heart flutters because he's in the room.

And then on his day,
He surprises me down on one knee
And asks for my hand
I'm so excited I'm shaking, I can barely stand

My heart is overwhelmed
God has blessed me beyond my dreams
With this man who may not be perfect
But God knows he's perfect for me.

Ours is a love story
Triumphant and bold
You are the love of my life
And you will forever occupy the space in my soul.

My heart is so full
Our love is impossible to contain
I will love you all the days in this life and the next…
Just the same.

My heart flutters as the butterflies in my stomach dance to our tune,
today is our wedding day, move closer, move closer…
My *husband* is in the room.

Reflections

Conversations from the White Sofa...

1. Make or (re-evaluate) your list!

2. If you are in a relationship, are you doing your part to ensure your relationship is successful? If not, what can you do to change that?

3. If you are looking for a relationship, what are you doing to ensure you are ready when God blesses you with a potential partner?

_____

_____

_____

_____

_____

_____

_____

_____

_____

_____

_____

_____

_____

_____

_____

_____

_____

_____

_____

_____

_____

"The Man ...
The Music ...
The Legend ..."

Chapter 4 ...
Prince of Hearts

To share a part of your soul is to allow someone to know you and to love that part of you.

This next series of works is my pause in time to pay tribute to, in my opinion, the greatest musician to ever live... Mr. Prince Rogers Nelson.

On this journey called life...Prince shared his soul with the world through his music.

We must all complete our journey here on earth. A journey that touches millions of souls is a journey well taken.

Such was his journey ...one well taken...

"Royalty"

Photo: Picture of a painting by Mel Brown McGinnis
Original Concept Design & Sketch: Buzzed Art Night &
Anita Mays, Eighty 8 Lines Art

My love of Prince and his music runs deep. I was surprised by my struggle to deal with his death because I didn't know him personally, but I felt his loss on such a deeply personal level. This is a photo of the piece that I painted at a "paint party" sponsored by Buzzed Art Nite about a month after his death. The photo is of a female … I named her "Royalty."

Rendition

"God has blessed me with the gift of words so I only hope I can do justice to the musical GENIUS that is ... Prince. At 11:20pm on 7.4.2014, the #Essencefest crowd screamed #Letsgocrazy as the #COOLest artist on the planet took the stage at the Louisiana Superdome. The crowd went wild and proclaimed please #Takemewithu on the baddest musical journey known to man! You "slowed down" in your #Littleredcorvette to whisper sweet sounds to the #Hotthing in the #Raspberryberet that only wants to live the #Glamorouslife. There was absolutely NO #Controversy because #Ugotthelook and at 56 there STILL #Aintnobodybadlikeu!!! It was so cold in the Superdome it felt like it was #Snowinginapril, lol!... but it didn't matter because we partied like it was #1999 and you were a #Dancingmachine killing it with moves only you can pull off. After an hour of dropping HITS, only you would ask the crowd if there were "any requests?" Lol! And since we couldn't make up our minds ...you #KISSed us with one more!!!! You are a showman, no doubt, popping out for surprise jam sessions with Nile Rodgers, blowing it out with Trombone Shorty, and sharing the stage with the beautiful Janelle Monae to make sure we were in full anticipation of your arrival. I knew it was a #SignOthetimes when you played another joint after a 10min 16sec absolute SLAYING of #Purplerain! You continuously shock the world and reinvent yourself and that piercing voice proves that your music will never leave us asking #Whathaveyoudoneformelately? You said #Letsfunk and the crowd followed your lead and provided the vocals for #Whendovescry. You spread mad #Junglelove and soared like #Thebird for nearly 2 hours all over the Superdome stage. You said "goodnight" at 1:05am, but the crowd refused to let you leave, after what was your second attempt at goodbye. So what did you do? You graciously hit the stage to give us more because we didn't want you to #Stopthemusic. Your release of 30 purple balloons into the night air was the culmination of 30 YEARS on top of the music game showing the world how it's done. After being blessed to hear your soaring vocals fill an arena for the 5th time live, I still know now what I knew then...#NOTHINGcompares2u!! So I simply say thank you for #theHITS Mr. Nelson ... they just keep on coming... #dropsthemic...close quotes... 1:13am..."

47

"Journey"
Photo: Lake Providence, Louisiana

This photo is of a bridge over historic Grant's Canal in Lake Providence, Louisiana. I took this picture on a photo tour of my hometown. Walking over a bridge symbolizes moving on to the next phase, crossing over to the other side, facing the next journey with your back to the past. In life's journey, we must all cross a bridge, and one day, we will all reach the other side...with our backs to the past...and our journey here on earth will be complete.

Rendition Complete

I cope with life through written words. I cope with death the same. Friday, April 22, 2016, will forever be the first day of the rest of my life... without Prince.

On Thursday, April 21, 2016, at 10:07 am, the world lost a musical genius, a humanitarian, a political activist, and a fashion icon...I lost my musical best friend... Prince Rogers Nelson, the man, the music, the legend...

Some might not understand how one could feel so close to someone they don't know personally, but Prince was literally one of my first loves, even before I understood what love was. Through his music, Prince shared a part of his soul. Even though I didn't know him personally, I knew the part of his soul that he wanted the world to know. Therefore, I knew a part of *him.*

For 5 days (but what seemed like an eternity to my heart) I could not find the words to express my thoughts or my feelings about the profound loss of this man that I did not know personally, but whose loss I felt on such a deeply personal level. Not only was I unable to express my thoughts, I could not even process the fact that the man and the music that I have loved since I was 8 years old (32 of my 40 years), the one whose music comforted me when there was no one else, the one whose music I related to like none other, the one who helped me understand myself when no one else understood, the one whose music I could rock out to one moment, and be all in my feelings about the next...was simply gone.

Loss of words is not something I suffer from so for me this was extremely critical. I have to admit that I was a bit annoyed by all of the "celebrations" and folks having "drinks to celebrate the purple one..." Not because I begrudge other people to celebrate in their own way and grieve in their own way and to honor his legacy and his music however they see fit, because like me, the world loved him too; but I was annoyed because I couldn't accept what they already had...that for all intents and purposes, one of the greatest loves of my life...was gone. I couldn't accept it, didn't want to accept it, so I wasn't ready to "celebrate his life" after death because I simply still wanted him here ... on this side of Heaven. I wanted to see more of him in concert (beyond the 5 times I had already been blessed to see him live) because he is the ONLY artist that I would pay almost any amount of money and travel just about anywhere to see live in concert; I wanted to continue to see him make impromptu appearances at awards shows; I was looking forward to his memoirs; I wanted to see him court side at basketball games;

I wanted to see more of that sly smile, gorgeous face, and seemingly unaging profile...I just simply wanted more.

When I was finally able to have a conversation about this massive loss that just broke my heart, I was speaking with a dear friend of mine (who also shares my love for my Prince) who helped me to see that I was having a hard time accepting this ...but it wasn't about me...it was about him. In my realization of my selfishness, I wasn't as hard on myself as I normally would have been for being selfish. I cut myself a little slack because I realized...I was grieving a profound loss and this was just a stage that I had to go through to get to where I am now. I know that he would want us to celebrate his life and his music.

So on day 5, I'm in the state of acceptance and I'm doing all I know how to do to cope... write until something comes out. So what follows is my account of the beginning of the rest of my life...without my Prince... and my open heart tribute to honor his life, his music and his legacy... This is my love letter ... to Prince.

Day 1...

As the world was shocked by your untimely departure, your fans took to the streets, social media, tv, radio and all things media to celebrate your life and the legacy of your music. Cities, states and even countries went "purple" in your honor.

Among the most famous were the Eiffel Tower, Niagra Falls, the London Eye, Chicago River, Empire State Building, Twin Cities Bridge in Your beloved Minneapolis/St Paul, and your home away from home, the Louisiana Superdome...even the Dallas Skyline went purple! You would have loved it!

Your fans lined the streets of Minneapolis and sang your songs all night. People all over the world held "Prince" parties and played your music to no end. News outlets, tv stations, Internet and radio stations quickly aired specials in your honor, played your entire catalogue of music from A-W (there are no songs that start with X, Y or Z), had video marathons, played Purple Rain on a non-stop loop, even movie theaters held special screenings of the pop culture iconic movie that vaulted your star into the stratosphere as you correctly proclaimed #BabyImAStar!! Musicians, actors and athletes alike took to social media to pay tribute to your legacy and your music... even Springsteen opened his Saturday night concert with Purple Rain. But the world should know that you were about more than just the music. You were a mentor to numerous artists, a friend to many many communities and educational institutions through your social and financial support, and an activist for a people who need a voice. You took a stand against the machine (record industry) and changed the game for artists 4ever. You spoke out and held special concerts when the races in this country once again were at a divide in cities like #Baltimore.

It was abundantly clear that you are respected, admired, loved and revered by so many people, including many musicians who are legends in their own right. Through your music and the world's love for you, you accomplished in one day, what world leaders have been trying to do for decades...bring the world together on one "purple" accord. In one day, your music sales went through the roof, literally you sold 1million songs and 231thousand albums...after death...I say that's a baaaaddddd man!... and a testament to your greatness.

Day 2...

As the world donned the color purple in your honor (one reporter even remarked that you OWN that color!) shock waves of disbelief and the simultaneous conflicting need to celebrate U continued to resonate. As I still struggled with acceptance of your passing, I can't let this rendition be spoken without explaining the personal nature of this loss to me. When I was 8 years old, my aunt (who shall rename nameless but I do love her so :) took me to see Purple Rain at the movie theatre. During the summer of 1984, again as an 8 year old, I can remember seeing the "uncut" version of Purple Rain....and I remember the music, and absolutely LOVING the music!! ...this was the day I fell in love with the musical genius that is Prince...

Also as an 8 year old, I was a member of the "Satin Dolls," a small girls dance group, and we did a dance routine to "Erotic City" in purple satin jackets with white lace trim...again, being too young to understand the lyrics, but just knew that I LOVED that music and your voice! In 1985, a little older now, and a majorette in the band (in a town and at a time when they let little girls be majorettes for a high school band) and we had a fabulous routine for homecoming and the Christmas parade to the Prince-penned cult hit "Glamorous Life" and again I loved LOVED the music. By then I was insanely hooked on music, and in particular, your music. Also that year my world was dominated by #RaspberryBeret, because that's all I wanted for my birthday that year was a raspberry beret, and my older cousin played #PopLife for me just about every day...

The year is now 1986 and #UnderTheCherryMoon was all the rage! Lol...that movie was suspect (well except for that moment when You do a half pirouette to that crazy drum beat at Mary Sharon's party wearing that black lace outfit with wave curls on the side of your face and I thought I was going to pass out!) .... Side note: I won't comment too much on your insanely gorgeous face but I have to mention that again here just to make sure you know :) ... again the movie was questionable, but the music, oh the music on that soundtrack was UNREAL!!!! #Kiss #Mountains #GirlsAndBoys #AnotherLoverHoleInYourHead (loved that yellow suit) ...and the list goes on and on...

Then at age 12, in 1987, for the first time with my own money that I had been saving for 3 months, I purchased my first cassette tape... it was a double album, #SignOTheTimes....and it was all over because that album boasted AMAZING jams that are too numerous to list here but also the one song that would become my favorite song off that album, or any album...EVER AND TO THIS DAY IS STILL MY ALL TIME FAVORITE SONG... #Adore...and the many many years that followed and the many albums and songs that I loved to no end but won't name them all, but I continued to love you ... and your music became the soundtrack of my life!!! I will take a moment at some point to name my top 100 favorite songs... cause I could never choose just 10, or 20 or even 30 of your #OldFriendsForSale...

Just a few words on the many times I was blessed to see you live and hear that amazing God-given voice of yours pierce the night air of any 10x1000 seat stadium. The first time was in 1997 for the #JamOfTheYear tour...I was gifted with a flight and tickets to see you at the Hollywood Bowl in Los Angeles for my birthday... wow! I shared that night with one of my cousins, who also shares my love for you. What a night...you donned that gorgeous red jumpsuit and the most memorable moment was seeing you descend off of your piano down to the stage in a full split and jump up and keep going! (I knew one day this would be a problem but wanted to enjoy that moment that night). In 2002 I had the privilege of spending #OneNightAlone with you at the Music Hall in Fair Park...I will never forget that day because it was a rainy day in April and it was my cousin's bday...and on that day DFW was hit with a tornado!!! But no tornado would stop me from seeing my Prince live! (I continue to laugh at myself for this lol!) So yes, I went to that concert, alone, without a companion, 2 hours after a tornado, but that didn't matter to me. I was going to see my Prince, so I knew I wouldn't be alone...and I wasn't...the concert was still sold out and the NPGMusicClub fam was in the building!!! In 2004ever along comes the famed #Musicology Tour...which you were jamming like none other! I ended up with THREE Musicology CDs (one I purchased and two from concerts) because you had the ingenious idea of giving every ticket holder for that tour a CD, thereby MASSIVELY increasing your sales. I was blessed to see you twice that year...once in Dallas, and as you headlined the 10 year anniversary of the #Essencefestival ... because no, I never EVER got tired of seeing you live!

10 years would go by before I was graced to be in your presence again, but what a time it was...it was 2013 and the girls and I had decided we were not going to Essence that next year, but then we found out you were coming and that was that...we sprung into action buying tickets online, booking flights and hotel in a matter of minutes. Our next jam session with the Purple One was booked! And of course you NEVER disappoint ... and July 4, 2014 owes me nothing! You rocked the Superdome that night!! So much so that I wrote "Rendition" in your honor. I thought I would be able to see you in concert for many years to come, but little did I know that would be the last time I would be blessed to hear your amazing vocals and watch you work a crowd like only you could!!! Thank you for that night Mr. Nelson. Thank you for the memories. I will never ever forget.

Day 3...

By Saturday April 23rd, only the memories and the music remained. Your vessel was cared for according to your faith and a private celebration of your life was held in your honor. Your staff distributed beautiful purple boxes filled with memorabilia (t-shirts, CDs, memory books, and the like) to your devoted fans who gathered outside your Paisley Park studios to honor your memory. As true fans can probably imagine, these were likely your last wishes... to honor your fans with gifts, and go quickly and quietly...in death just as you lived life.

Your life is complete, your work here on #PlanetEarth is done. The number 7 is given the distinction of the number of completion in the Bible. Like one of the most prolific songs ever written #7... "All seven and we'll watch them fall..."

Your earthly journey began on the 7th day of June, and came to an end at the age of 57 at 10:07am... but your life and your legacy will live on...

What I know for sure is that God gifted us with such a rare and beautiful life that through your immense God-given talent and quiet storm spirit you have touched so many and blessed so many with your voice, your music and your generosity. God allowed us to borrow you for a few years and has allowed you to fulfill your true purpose to impact the world, as only He knew you would.

God bless you my dear Prince. May your soul be at rest and at peace eternally with your parents, your son, and our Heavenly Father. You have gained your 27 golden instruments, and soon there will be a new city with streets of gold... and Best of all I know that tonight and every night 4ever will be a #BeautifulNight because undoubtably you are the #JamOfThe-Year up there in Heaven for 2016 and there has to be an UNDENIABLE jam session with guitars, pianos, snare drums and horns ablazing going on in Heaven right now!!!

You are STILL and ALWAYS will be the BADDEST musician this side of Heaven...and your legacy and musical genius will live on 4ever... So #DanceOn my Prince...I will simply say goodnight, but never goodbye.

...I wish u love, #IWishUHeaven, I wish U Heaven, Mr. Nelson.

Prince Rogers Nelson ~ June 7, 1958 – Infinity

"Tunnel Vision"
Photo: Underground tunnel outside Paisley Park Studios
Chanhassen, Minnesota
(Tunnel Painting: Artist Unknown)

No tribute to Prince is complete without a trip to the motherland… the hallowed grounds of Paisley Park. My husband surprised me with tickets for the VIP Tour of Paisley Park! Touring the mythical palace that I have known (in my mind) for most of my life was simply surreal. I was "at home" in a place I had never physically been. This is a photo of my husband and I in the underground tunnel which has become a haven of tributes to Prince, including the painting on the top of the tunnel, which is a creation using the famous symbol synonymous with Prince himself!

My Purple Heart

The magic of a surreal heart is to allow you to be "at home" in a place you've never been.

... my purple heart is bursting still...this is my attempt to memorialize the AMAZING sights I was blessed to behold on Sunday, October 29, 2017, at the one and only PAISLEY PARK STUDIOS in Chanhassen, Minnesota... music studio and home to his "Royal Badness" Mr. Prince Rogers Nelson...many of the rooms preserved just as he left them... home is where the purple heart is....

THE ENTRANCE - you enter the building to Raspberry Beret-like clouds that run the height of the staircase with murals of Prince on either side of the entrances and the ceiling lined with piano keys. The stairwell boasts the Purple One's many platinum and gold records enclosed in glass casings, including a life size collection of tickets from EVERY stop on the Musicology tour that is called the "Musicology Wheel" as it is in the shape of a wheel. To the left of the entrance hallway sits a letter signed in purple ink from Barack and Michelle Obama expressing their condolences to the Paisley Park family and Prince fans around the world. Also a posthumously awarded American Music Award for Purple Rain for Best soundtrack as album sales went through the roof after his passing. The coolest part about the entrance is when you look straight ahead you see Prince's beautiful eyes looking back at you!

THE ATRIUM - I got very emotional here. This area is open space and the Love Symbol adorns the white ceramic tiled floor in the middle of the room. There are 4 pyramid shaped sky lights in the middle of the atrium that allow tons of natural light to come through. The purple lights can be activated to shine bright and light the sky purple at night. The ceiling is painted with doves flying to the top of the sky lights. Paisley Park is also home to 3 live doves that live in a cage on the 2nd floor. The atrium is also appropriately Prince's final resting place as his ashes sit atop the perch of the atrium in a frosted glass case with the love symbol on the outside. We had to pause here for a moment ... tears flowed... too many emotions to tell you. To the left of the atrium area are walk-in closets wallpapered with Prince photos and quotes from his favorite lyrics. The area holds many of Prince's guitars, and each closet represents an album, including the actual outfits that Prince wore in the videos for that album. Each video from that album played on the screen. To the right of the atrium was his very own café, complete with booth seating, a microwave to enjoy the popcorn he would love to come down and pop, and a large television overhead to watch all of the basketball games that he so loved!

Side Note: I've seen Prince in concert many times and 3 of those shows I had AWESOME seats so I had the chance to get a great view of him, but I never had the opportunity to actually meet him in person. I say that to say I have a new appreciation for his small yet powerful stature lol! Those outfits were almost doll like! I couldn't imagine gaining 10 pounds... my goodness you would have to replace the entire wardrobe! ... I digress...

HIS OFFICE - The Office is on the main level with the standard items but extremely unique and "made for Prince"... the sofa... not just any sofa... but a purple valor chase lounge lol! On the "Prince-sized" desk sits a purple phone and candles adorn the office (by the way the ENTIRE place is adorned with candles in almost every room-although the real fire burning candles have been replaced with battery operated ones for museum purposes). His copy of the commemorative collection from the O2 concerts sits in a massive purple bound album on top of a column. Also present are photos of family and friends on a small table in front of the window. A stack of books sit next to the black piano topped with the Oxford Bible, books about Egypt and astronomy. On the conference table sit sketches of the album cover Prince and his team were working on at the time of his passing. An overnight bag and a computer bag sit to the left of the desk.

THE CUTTING ROOM - This room gave the appearance of what us normal folk would call a media room, but it is the video editing room. It was set up theatre style but only had one sofa, a small coffee table, a large tv screen, and a computer/editing board. The tour guide indicated this is where all of Prince's footage was edited. Apparently he was fanatical about recording every rehearsal, concert, interview, performance etc. If

58

a performance didn't live up to his standard, it would quite often end up on the cutting room floor. We viewed a video that was edited in the room.

THE O2 GUITAR - Prince had a guitar commissioned by a guitar maker in England while he was there doing the 21 shows at the O2. The guitar was made especially for him, but due to miscommunication through the years, he didn't receive the guitar until March 2016. It is a beautiful purple guitar trimmed in gold. He loved it so much he commissioned the guitar maker to make him a matching bass guitar. Sadly he never got a chance to play the guitar and he never got the bass guitar. **Appropriately, Bruno Mars now has the bass (more on Bruno later lol!)**

THE MOVIE THEMED ROOMS – Paisley Park boasted many rooms that were themed from some of Prince's movies. Familiar outfits that Prince donned in the video or the accompanying movie also graced the room. "Under the Cherry Moon" was highlighted by the video for "Mountains" playing on the screen; Sign "O" the Times… the live concert; "Graffiti Bridge," well let's just say the music was always the best thing about this one; and of course, the Royal High of "Purple Rain" boasted its own space – the Motorcycle that Prince rode throughout the movie was nestled inside of a ringed area that of course was "do not touch;" the script for the movie sat on top of a column in a purple leather bound book like a purple bible nestled on the pew; the famous purple jacket and white layered shirt from the final scene was the featured outfit; the Oscar for Best Original Score was also on display; the movie "Purple Rain" played on the video wall; and the coolest feature was these items were encased in a mural that matches the artwork from the backside of the Purple Rain album sleeve!

BRUNCH IN THE NPG MUSIC CLUB – One of the highlights of the tour was our very own brunch in the NPG Music Club room. This room was used as the gathering haven for late night jam sessions, impromptu concerts and other large gatherings. We were greeted by Prince's chefs, who made us one of his favorite meals – scrambled eggs with red peppers and avocado slices, roasted potatoes, cinnamon toast topped with chocolate spread and fresh squeezed orange juice.

OTHER C.O.O.L. SPACES AND PLACES - Paisley Park is home to Prince's *Inspiration and Influence Hallway,* which is a mural the length of the entire hallway inspired by the likes of Larry Graham, Stevie Wonder, Chaka Khan, James Brown, The Staple Singers, Joni Mitchell and Sly and the Family Stone. These are the artists that Prince was influenced and inspired by in his music. *Awards Row* is a full length hallway with all of Prince's awards housed in glass casings, including Grammy Awards, American Music Awards, BET Awards, and many more. Oh and *The Sound Stage* is absolutely AMAZING!!! The entrance to the Sound Stage is the photo of the eyes staring at you on the Purple Rain album sleeve ☺ …Sign "O" the Times and Graffiti Bridge were largely filmed here…and the Sound Stage houses two of Prince's baddest rides …a timeless Bentley and a rare Prowler! *Studio B i*s where the "magic happens!" Many a hit were recorded in this studio by many famous artists, including Madonna, Paula Abdul, Tevin Campbell, Mavis Staples and the list goes on and on. Studio B is also home to Prince's purple baby grand, table tennis where my tour mates and I were blessed to be able to play a few games (and where, according to the tour guide, Bruno and the Houligans also played a mean game of ping pong on their tour!). This studio is the one and only location in the entire building where photos are allowed (and only in the designated spot next to the wall sized mural of Prince, and only taken by the tour guide), but they are still to be cherished nonetheless lol!

This pilgrimage is a must for any true fan of this musical genius!

ℛ*eflections*

Conversations from the White Sofa...

1. If you're a Prince fan, I will give you a moment to breathe... if you're not a Prince fan, I hope this chapter at least gives you a new appreciation for his music and his legacy.

2. Who is your favorite musical artist? What is your favorite musical genre?

3. What role, if any, does music play in your life to lift your spirits and/or lighten your mood?

_____

_____

_____

_____

_____

_____

_____

_____

_____

_____

_____

_____

_____

_____

_____

_____

_____

_____

_____

_____

_____

_____

"America the Beautiful."

Chapter 5 ... This America

The heights in life to which you rise are not determined by where you begin...you can have roots and wings...

That is of course the basic tenant of this country that we call America.

Somewhere deep in the annals of my mind, I still have the audacity to hope that someday "this" America might in reality, mirror its ideals.

"The View From Here"
Photo: The Lake — Lake Providence, Louisiana

I wrote this poem as a tribute to my roots. I spent my formative teenage years growing up in Monroe, Louisiana, but I was born in a small town in northeast Louisiana called Lake Providence and grew up there through middle school. This poem is an honest tribute to a family oriented town that was (and still is) divided by this beautiful lake, literally and figuratively. The lake was the dividing line between black and white, rich and poor, the haves and the have nots. Even though many of us grew up in what fits America's definition of poor, you wouldn't know it because our lives were rich with love, laughter, faith, family tradition, and the belief that if you worked hard, and trusted in God's plan for your life, you could be successful no matter where you came from.

Providence

the view from here
what do I see?

imagine a massive body of water
a lake that divides you and me

one side of the lake is riddled with poverty
where windows are boarded

and the floors of homes cave in
dilapidation is the norm

and the mentality of the housing projects serves as the home from
within

there exists but two stop lights in the entire town

you can go from new town to
across the tracks in one fail swoop without making a sound

the view from here
what do I see?

i see a body of water
a lake that divides you and me

one side is riddled with poverty
the other with prosperity

while Mandy rides to the Academy in her Mercedes Benz
and lives her life with ease

my sisters and I stand in line at the Council on Aging
to collect our powdered milk and government cheese

i was not allowed to attend Mandy's school
she wouldn't be caught dead on my side of the trees

late to bloom in 1980

this small town
with a population of six thousand plus three

as a child of 5 years of age
when desegregation had just recently come to be

i was bussed to the school called northside
to get the better education
they said only you could provide

"across the lake" as it was called
that mythical place
that only the well-off saw

our lives divided by the lake
literally and figuratively

my idea of a summer job
was working as a hand in the cotton field of dreams

a place called providence
once was a bustling cultural center of the south

you might be surprised to know that
the mighty Mississippi River runs through it and around

the mere definition of providence
God shines light on His own

the protective care of His spiritual nature
a place with powers unknown

a place where Easter Sunday speeches, talent shows and homecoming
parades were all the rage

a place where we celebrated miss 3rd
miss 4th and miss 5th grade

majorettes and satin dolls
dance into the night

as the Panthers step on the field
to the hometown fans' delight
divine providence is that from which my guidance comes
a place and a people that God selected as the chosen ones

we were small yet mighty
literally the poorest town in America
once said TIME Magazine

but to little black girls and boys with big dreams
the elders would say "you can have roots and wings"

fate, destiny, divine intervention
call it what you like

it was our intention
to show the world that our view is pure and good
and an honorable mention is a slight

a place where grandmothers, aunts, uncles and cousins
sit outside and revel in the moonlight

where the kids catch lightning bugs
until the street lights burn yellow and bright

where the choirs would march from the back of the church singing "go
tell it on the mountain" high

where the natives return each year to celebrate history
and success stories cannot be denied

a place where everyone
knows everyone else

where your children are my children
and we all give of ourselves

to make our view from here
one we can all be proud of

lake providence is what we call it
rooted in family, draped in love

some of our own once burned the high school
rich with tradition

but that didn't hold us down
we rebuilt and continued the mission

it's no mistake that from this small town hails
some of the most brilliant minds
let me tell you

of senators, artists, educators, CEO's and professional athletes too,
doctors, lawyers, nurses and the good men and women that wear the
blue

writers, economists, mayors, principals, coaches and those who take
flight

technology professionals, singers, project managers, counselors and
business owners alike

we are small yet mighty
so never count us out

many were baptized in the waters of the lake
under the cover of divine providence, no doubt

we have made our view from here
one we are all proud of

lake providence is what we call it
rooted in family, draped in love.

The Color of Success

The Color of Success rings true for such a small town that has produced greatness of so many. I am so proud to share the success stories of these beautiful ladies from my home town and the many chosen fields and careers of others who hail from the field of dreams!!!

Lynda Bunch Carmouche
Licensed Pscychotherapist,
Licensed Social Worker, Author,
Playright, Empowerment Speaker
BS Social Work; MS Social Work

Jeslyn Lewis
Author, Writer, Playright,
Advocate Against Domestic Violence
Regional Outreach Prevention
Coordinator

Angela Butler Lewis
Regional Credit Manager, Credit &
Collections Expert, BS Computer
Information Systems;
MS Business Administration

Tabitha Wilson McDowell
Mental Health Program Specialist and
future Employee Relations Manager BS
Office Administrations; MA Candidate

Pamela Wright Honoré
Licensed Professional Counselor,
Behavioral Health Program Manager &
Photographer
BS Psychology; MA Mental Health
Counseling
Doctoral Candidate,
Developmental Psychology

Latayatacha Ross
Nurse Practitioner, APRN-FNP
BS Nursing; MS Nursing

Jayadra Henderson Rodney
Math Instructional Specialist
BS Mathematics;
MEd Educational Leadership

We are LP!

Retired Navy Computer Specialist

Photographer

*Educator *Computer Engineer *Chef*

*Grant Writer *Licensed Nurse Practitioner*

*Photographer *Sr Construction Field Technician*

*Attorney * Minister*

*School Resource Officer *Gospel Recording Artist*

Licensed Professional Counselor

Pre-Doctoral Candidate

* Doctorally-prepared RN and future Nurse Anesthetist*

*Legal Secretary *Business Owner *Court Clerk*

*Magazine Editor and CEO   *Vice President Strategy & M&A*

*Criminal Investigator *Licensed Cosmetologist *

Sheriff

*Licensed Insurance Broker *Commercial Vehicle Driver*

Corporate Trainer of Digital Finance

Correctional Officer

*Public Housing Program Manager *

Film Director/Producer

*Master Fitness Trainer *Assistant Principal *Veteran*

"Field of Dreams"
Photo: Cotton field outside of Providence, LA

As a child growing up in a small town in Louisiana, my sister and I worked as field hands in the cotton fields during the summer with our great aunt and grandfather. To get through my time from 6am to 12noon, I would dream of all the things I wanted to do in life. I look at the inauguration of President Barack Obama as the realization of Martin Luther King, Jr's dream that one day we would all be judged not by the color of our skin, but by the content of our character. That we would all be created equal. I began writing this poem on January 21, 2013, which was MLK day and also the day of the 2nd Inauguration of President Obama. I decided to wait until after President Obama's second term to complete this piece. What follows is my tribute to President Obama in the likeness of Dr. Martin Luther King, Jr., and a testament to how far we've come, but also an acknowledgment of how far we still have yet to go.

Of Kings and Presidents

Today we honor a man named King,
For the second time we realize *his* dream
Through the inauguration of an American President
Not just any President, the people's President, it would seem

A President who has borne the sharp tongue of hate
Withstood the disrespectful tenor of these divided states
It is of Kings and Presidents that we speak
Mr. 44 who hails from the field of dreams

Grandmother never thought she would see the day
When a man who looked like her
Would be leading the way

Leader of the free world
Opposition from all angles, the same as King
Yet the landslide victory was his to proclaim
Underhanded antics would not be his defeat

In spite of the race war
His very presence would surely incite
As crosses were burned and promises were made
To the rioters' delight

Promises to return to a time
When a man like King would be put in his place
Where the spirit crippling mindset of Jim Crow
Might threaten to seal his fate

But oh this President hails from the field of dreams
The enlightened America stood up to pay attention it seems
To a nation whose moral compass
Is compromised at best

But not all of us suffer from
The notion that the under privileged amongst us deserve less

Armed with an ivy league education
He would leave his impact on the stars and stripes
There was even a ludicrous challenge
To his birth right

This American President
Who an enlightened America elected once more
Whose family would once again
Gracefully occupy the upper room floor

There are those who want us to believe
It was 8 years of waste
Opposition at every turn
Let the record reflect that those who can't do…hate

Economy rising, took out Bin Laden
Bailed out the auto industry to boot
Even won the Nobel Peace Prize on the low
His biggest scandal … the *tan suit*

Mr. President, you did what 5 presidents before you
Could not do
Passed universal health care
Yeah you did that too

Renewed the GI bill for the veteran's support
It was a great day in the nation
When you put the 1st Hispanic woman
On the High Court

Recover and reinvest in America you said
You got us over the hump of recession
Cut homelessness in half
Protected the DREAMers on our land
And did I mention you taught Bin Laden a lesson?

You ended the nearly decade long military drain of Iraq
Reduced hate crimes, fair pay for the ladies, marriage for all
Wall Street was rescued on Dodd-Frank's back

As you left office, we were bursting with pride and joy
And at the same time relief
Eight years…attempts on your life no doubt…

None successful
Thankful this nation would not have to endure that grief

In spite of your record which will forever stand
Although you are your brother's keeper
It is painfully obvious that to some
That doesn't trump the fact that you're still a black man

Some will never give you credit
Your very existence still offends
So much so that half the nation turned a blind eye
And put 45 in office
In spite of his sins

It was in that moment of realization
My eyes swelled with tears
Because I knew then that history
Would be far kinder to you Sir
Than your peers…

But that, Mr. President, is neither here nor there
And oh the stories that we will share
We do not all still long for the days of Jim Crow
So we will write it down in history
And tell little boys and girls the stories of Mr. O

We will celebrate your victories
We will acknowledge the mysteries

Of how you were able to put down
Our one true enemy

We will tell them of your love for people
Black, white, yellow, brown, straight or gay
We will tell them about your undeniable swag
Your love for Mrs. O, and how she would always slay

We will not sit by idly
We will not let your legacy go quietly as night turns to day
We will celebrate the fact that you are and always will be
The 44th President of these United States

The twenty first of January, two thousand thirteen
A day America will not soon forget
Lest we will always remember the monumental struggle
Of kings and *field of dream* Presidents.

Reflections

Conversations from the White Sofa...

1. What can you do to encourage positive race relations in America?

2. Are you a small town success story, or do you know someone who is? What challenges do you think a person from a small, poor town faces in becoming successful in life?

3. What pathways to success have you identified in your career and what advice would you give to someone who is looking to find their way in your industry? Will you commit to mentoring a young person who is interested in your industry?

_____

_____

_____

_____

_____

_____

_____

_____

_____

_____

_____

_____

_____

_____

_____

_____

_____

_____

_____

_____

_____

"In Some Way, Whether We Want to Admit It or Not, We Are All Responsible for Each Other."

Chapter 6 ... My Brother ... My Sister ... My Keeper

The sad truth is that we have become desensitized to violence in America ...violence against women, senseless gun violence resulting in attacks on innocent children, the litany is lengthy.

If you know someone in an abusive relationship, if you are in an abusive relationship, or if you know someone who may be suffering from a mental illness, please seek help and don't ignore the signs. Your life, and the lives of others, really does depend on it.

We have to remedy the cause, in order to change the effect.

"Heaven's Gate"
Photo: Port of the Bahamas, Caribbean Sea

I wrote this next piece in honor of my sisters in love and all of the beautiful women who senselessly lost their lives to domestic violence. Sunset on the ocean is the most beautiful thing I've ever seen. I took this photo leaning over the railing on the side of a cruise ship in the port of Nassau. In my mind, Heaven must be like this. I would hope each of these amazing souls would see something this beautiful upon their entry into heaven's gates.

To Heaven's Angel

I woke up this morning and I can still see your face
Just as beautiful as the sunrise as night turned to day
Your heart and warmth transcended all things
Although you're no longer here on earth
Your life will forever bear mentioning

Today began without you
You've crossed over to the other side
But your smile, your grace, your laughter
Will always remain frozen in time

Sweet spirit on earth
Unforgettable you are
You touched the lives of so many
Your journey… so brief yet so far

In that fateful moment you saw unrecognizable rage
Though not likely the first time, this was a different stage
This time, you couldn't talk him down
This time, he wouldn't listen to reason
But this time, was *your* time
And God declared it was your season

Clothed in God's love
his cowardly act would not be the last thing you see
Because God protects His angels from chaotic insanity
God covered you with silence
Serenity and glowing warmth ever bold
Then allowed you to witness that awesome light
To greet your rescued soul

My sweet angel in Heaven
Scripture teaches revenge is not mine to seek

I choose to honor your memory
With love, laughter and in peace

You've gained your wings Heaven's angel
No longer paralyzed by fear or pain
Although I will miss you dearly
I know I will see you again

Take your place my sweet angel
Write your name across the sky
Continue to paint the golden roads
For I will cry neither tear nor sigh

I will smile each time I think of you
They will all know your name
Dance on in Heaven sweet angel
Until we meet again

Rest easy my beautiful angel
Your work here is done I'm told
Rest easy Heaven's angel
Eternity has claimed your soul.

*For Heaven's angels ... Aleria, Monica, Zina, Adrienne and all the other
  beautiful angels who have lost their lives senselessly to domestic violence.*

"Birds of a Feather"
Photo: Pink Flamingo, Tampa Zoo

I wrote this poem out of anger and sheer frustration of the number of shootings that have occurred in our country over the last few years, especially at schools. It perplexes me how we can effect change on so many levels through the legislative and executive processes, but we can't seem to stop automatic weapons from falling into the hands of domestic terrorists who commit mass murders against innocent US citizens...and I'm even more frustrated that our leadership largely chooses to blame the actions of these domestic terrorists on mental illness rather than calling it what it is... I chose this photo because all birds flock together, but they are not all the same... and they are not all crazy.

Crazy.has.a.name

Mental illness is real and should never be taken lightly. But to steal another person's joy simply because you can, is NOT crazy ... it's evil...

i want to scream
i want to cry
my heart breaks for this the only home
i've ever known...besides

why do we continue to allow
CRAZY to thrive?
we throw billions at walls
we throw millions at bans
but we can't seem to stop our
precious ones from falling to CRAZY'S hands.

my truth is muted...
my anger and frustration continue to rise
we stand by and do nothing
offering our obligatory thoughts and prayers
as we watch the news and cry

action is the need now
the time for lip service has passed
45 please don't let our precious ones
continue to fall at CRAZY'S hands.

don't let this be our new normal
you saw this coming
but protocols weren't followed
so again...you did nothing

CRAZY has a look

CRAZY has a name

he's no longer the face from the concrete jungle
CRAZY shows up at your neighborhood games.

if this land is your land, and also mine
why do some of us get beaten and banned
on instruction from the top man's dime?

don't call him CRAZY
CRAZY has a name
don't call him CRAZY
make him face the pain…

don't say he's CRAZY…

say he calculated
say he manipulated
say he pre-meditated
say he took the lives of innocent babies

but don't say he's CRAZY

don't give him a pass
hold him accountable
like you do every black man…and

if you make the gun laws in Amerika
you should be ashamed of yourself
CRAZY bought his AR-15
off the Internet.

So don't call him CRAZY
call him by his name…
say he calculated
say he manipulated
say he pre-meditated

say he took the lives of innocent babies…

HE'S NOT INSANE…so don't call him CRAZY

he has a name…
call him Dylann
call him Adam
call him Devin
call him James

call him Omar
call him Stephen
call him Micah
call him Nikolus to date…

CRAZY has a look
CRAZY has a name

it's homegrown…terrorist…radical…SANE.

Reflections

Conversations from the White Sofa...

1. Can you identify the warning signs of domestic violence?

2. Are you, or someone you know, a victim of domestic violence or suffering from a mental illness? If yes, what can you do to get out of the situation, or what can you do to help someone else? Are you aware of resources that may be used to assist?

3. Do you know your elected officials? If you answered no, please do the research to find out. What plan of action can you put in place to contact your local, state and federally elected officials to encourage them to propose or support laws to prevent and/or reduce domestic violence and gun violence in this country? What will your proposal include?

_____
_____
_____
_____
_____
_____
_____
_____
_____
_____
_____
_____
_____
_____
_____
_____
_____
_____
_____

"Athletes Don't Compete Against Other Athletes... They Compete Against Perfection."

Chapter 7 ... The Game

*One of the greatest displays of discipline you will ever see
is in an elite athlete...sports is the great equalizer...
because competitive sport is the one arena in which victory
isn't given to you...*

*it is the thing you must earn...
to be a lover of sports ... is to live and die
for the passion of competition.*

"Passion"
Photo: Island of Co Co Cay, Bahamas

This is one of my favorite photos from my *Natural Elements* collection because it screams passion...I took this photo on the beach in Co Co Cay and I love it because it's so bright, and vibrant, and exciting! This is exactly how I feel when I'm entrenched in the throws of a great game or match... and my favorite player or team is in the hunt for the win...I'm competitive by nature, and sports is food for my soul!

FANatic

No offering from me would be complete without letting you in on my love of sports! I am the biggest sports *FAN*atic I know…there are so many stories I could tell you about my love of sports, but I've chosen to share how it all began…that moment when I knew.

The first time I experienced heart break was in 1992 when my high school football team lost the state championship game by a field goal after an undefeated season. I had never cried like that before. The pain was deeply felt and gut wrenching. That season had been one for the record books with a senior laden varsity squad that had been playing together since they were in eighth grade. I had the pleasure of cheering them on in my black and gold uniform that year as a member of the famed Tigerette pep-squad. That team boasted the top-ranked defense in the state, "law dawgs" we called them. We were so close to victory we could all taste it; but as the story began, you know that didn't happen.

That was the first time I experienced heart break, and that's when I knew that my first love, wasn't the 6'1, 220 pound all-state linebacker that I used to date…*it was football.*

"Alaskan Beauty"
Photo: Anchorage, Alaska

I chose this photo because this sight has to be the clearest Natural Element I have ever laid eyes on. I took this photo during an Alaskan cruise. This sight was so beautiful it was hard to believe my eyes that this was right in front of me. I imagine that an athlete in the zone is experiencing the most clarity he or she has ever experienced, when all things come together for that perfect moment in time. That is what this beautiful Alaskan mountain represents…perfect clarity.

To The Athlete in The Zone

To the Athlete in the Zone:

What is it like to be in the Zone?

Does the 18-inch hoop appear as wide as the ocean?

Does the defense part like the red sea when you run for 43 yards on a 4th and 1 with 20 seconds left on the first Sunday in February?

Does the small of the bat feel as powerful as a hydraulic powered rocket launching your three-run homer into the October sky?

What is it like to be in the Zone?

Adrenalin pumping…hands sweating
Dilated pupils magnify the incoming light around you…

If you're in the Zone
You must not miss
You don't miss
You can't miss…

By all counts…you *must* be in the Zone.

When you're in the Zone,

You bowl a score of 285
You pitch a no-hitter in Yankee Stadium
You shoot a 69 on moving day with an eagle on 17 as you flash the familiar fist pump into the air …

You demolish your opponent one & love
On the hallowed grass of Centre Court at the All England Club in July,

as you let out the primal scream of "c'mon!"
When you're in the Zone
You must not miss
You don't miss
You can't miss....

You *must* be in the Zone ... again.

I'm no athlete
But I do *know* athletes
So maybe at the very least, I can *recognize* "The Zone"
As your biggest *FAN*atic
I am most in love with you
When you are in the Zone...

I cheer you on because I can't believe you made that shot
You throw it up from anywhere...even half court
And it goes in...*swish*!!!
You float outside of your body
You don't hear the crowd roar
As you sink your sixth three-point basket in row

Yet the net remains still...

The thrill of competition makes your heart race
120 miles per hour
As the white flag waves you around the last turn at the 500

Adrenalin pumping...hands sweating
Your face flush red from labored breathing

You must not miss
You don't miss
You can't miss...

By all counts...you *are* in the Zone.

Your opponent tries his level best
To simply disrupt your game
But he knows what you and I know too…
That tonight…he can't stop you
He can only hope to contain you…

You *will* make that shot
You *will* complete that 38-yard pass for the touchdown
Again…because we all knew it was coming…
The FANatics called your number before the coach did

So you must not miss
You don't miss
You can't miss…

You are in the Zone…again.

So to the athlete in the Zone

I salute you
You are in that perfect space
Where the sun, the moon and the stars have aligned
You have achieved nirvana…

You are at the top of the Game…

And you must not miss
You don't miss
You can't miss…

The paint must look like a parking lot as you go up for the slam dunk…
your opponent just got posterized!

You are in the Zone…again.

Who's next?

Conversations from the White Sofa...

1. What role does sports play in our society? What values can our children learn from playing sports?

2. Do we place too much emphasis on sports for our children?

3. In your opinion, is there more or less emphasis placed on sports than on education in our country?

4. If you see this as a problem, what is your solution?

_____

_____

_____

_____

_____

_____

_____

_____

_____

_____

_____

_____

_____

_____

_____

_____

_____

_____

_____

_____

_____

_____

_____

"You Can't Choose
Your Family ...
But You Can Choose
To Forgive ... and Love
Them Anyway."

Chapter 8 ... Family Ties

*I've seen many faces in life staring back at me...
but not the one I wanted to see. The love of family is
ultimately what makes the world go round.*

*To be missing that part of your life, where you have an
absent, or mostly absent parent, can leave you
feeling empty and regretful at times.*

*But life is about playing the hand you're dealt and not
using that absenteeism as a crutch or an excuse for not
succeeding.*

"Perennials in Bloom"
Photo: Mt. Alyeska, Anchorage, Alaska

As I look into the scenic wilderness highlighted by the perennials in bloom, I see many faces of life staring back at me…but not the one I want to see. My mother did an amazing job raising four girls, largely on her own. I grew up without my father as a consistent part of my life. For years, I longed for a relationship with my father but rarely did I see his face…eventually, I just saw my own face…and realized that was enough.

Faces of Life

It's tomorrow again and the sun also rises
I awake the same as yesterday
And only your reflection remains
I arrived in this world not long ago
Yet today I stare at the ceiling
And wonder what *this* day will bring
Your face is burned into my memory
No voice, no laugh, no words, no expression, just your face.

It's tomorrow again and the sun also rises
Everything reminds me of you today
Today is the day I graduate from high school
Seventh in my class
So one would think that was special
But I only see your fading reflection today
No voice, no laugh, no words, no expression, just your face.

It's tomorrow *again* and the sun also rises
I see my mother's face today,
but you're not at her side
Today is the day I graduate from college
First in my family to graduate from such an institution
So one would think *that* was special
But I only see your faded reflection

No voice, no laugh, no words, no expression, just your face.

It's tomorrow again and the sun also rises
I see *your* mother's face today,
but you're not at *her* side either.

Today is the day I graduate from law school
First in my family to join the ranks of such a profession

So one would think *that* was special
But today, I don't even see your reflection.

I can't remember your voice, or your laugh, or your words, or your expression, not even your face.
It's tomorrow again and the sun has risen
Life has been good to me even without your face.

Today is the day I become a wife,
So one would think *that* was special
Only today, today I do see your face, though not too familiar
I hear your voice, I hear your laugh, I hear your words, I see your expression, I even see your face, though it doesn't move me that you're here.

The sun rose again this morning, but today,
I only see my face…and I now know… that is enough.

…I am enough.

Reflections

Conversations from the White Sofa...

1. Is there a family relationship you would like to improve or repair?

2. Is forgiveness required on your part?

3. What steps will you take and what specific things will you commit to doing in order to improve or repair the relationship?

_____

_____

_____

_____

_____

_____

_____

_____

_____

_____

_____

_____

_____

_____

_____

_____

_____

_____

_____

_____

_____

_____

_____

_____

"Envision the Life You Want. Plan For It, Work For It, and Make It Happen!"

Chapter 9 ... Your Reflections

Reflection ... to be in thought, meditation, deliberation, introspection, quiet contemplation...

This chapter will provide you an opportunity to take a few moments to reflect on the moments that have shaped your life.

Reflection is important...and it is good for the soul!

Your Reflections

I am honored that you stayed this course with me to the end of this journey. I hope that you have connected with the works in this collection in some way, and that this will help you on your own journey. Life is fleeting, and precious, and God blesses each of us with a purpose in life. We must live each day out loud, with intention...and work to fulfill that purpose every day that we are blessed to *breathe.*

Find that thing in life that moves you...
and then dance for it!

Whether you are reading this collection individually or with a group, the pages that follow are meant to be used to write down *your* Reflections of Life.

1. Which chapter(s) in this collection did you connect with the most and why?
2. What are your top 5 goals in life? What are you doing, or what will you do to achieve those goals?
3. What are you passionate about, i.e. what makes you dance? What will you do to pursue that passion?
4. What's on your bucket/basket list? (I don't do buckets) lol!

Reflections

Reflections

"Live Your Life Out Loud...On Purpose... and With Purpose!"

~

Always,
Mel

About The Author

Mel Brown McGinnis is a renowned author and poet who has been writing poetry and prose since childhood. She received her Bachelor's Degree in English Literature and her Juris Doctorate from Louisiana State University. She is a licensed attorney and certified sports agent, but feels most at home when she is dabbling in all things creative.

Mel enjoys music, dancing, photography, shopping, traveling, scrapbooking, planning weddings, and running. When she's not on the move or enjoying one of her many hobbies, she can be found catching episodes of her favorite soap operas and TV shows from the 80's. Mel is happily married, and lives by the mantra that successful people in life are the best at living life out loud…on purpose and with purpose!

Made in the USA
Lexington, KY
12 October 2018